T0081022

JOURNEY TO AMERICA

A Chronology of Immigration in the 1900s

by Danny Kravitz

Consultant:
Cindy R. Lobel, PhD
Associate Professor of History
Lehman College
Bronx, New York

CAPSTONE PRESS
a capstone imprint

Connect Books are published by Capstone Press,
1710 Roe Crest Drive, North Mankato, Minnesota 56003
www.capstonepub.com

Library of Congress Cataloging-in-Publication Data
Kravitz, Danny, 1970–
Journey to America : a chronology of immigration in the 1900s / by Danny Kravitz.
pages cm.—(Connect. U.S. immigration in the 1900s)
     Summary: "Explores the waves of immigration into the United States in the early
1900s"—Provided by publisher.
Includes bibliographical references and index.
     ISBN 978-1-4914-4126-8 (library binding)
     ISBN 978-1-4914-4172-5 (pbk.)
     ISBN 978-1-4914-4178-7 (ebook pdf)
     ISBN 978-1-4914-7889-9 (reflowable epub)
1. European Americans—History—19th century—Juvenile literature. 2. European
Americans—History—20th century—Juvenile literature. 3. Immigrants—History—
19th century—Juvenile literature. 4. Immigrants—History—20th century—Juvenile
literature. 5. United States—Emigration and immigration—History—19th century—
Juvenile literature. 6. United States—Emigration and immigration—History—20th
century—Juvenile literature. 7. Europe—Emigration and immigration—History—19th
century—Juvenile literature. 8. Europe—Emigration and immigration—History—
20th century—Juvenile literature. I. Title.
E184.E95K73 2016
304.8'407309034—dc23   2015004534

Editorial Credits
Jen Besel and Mandy Robbins, editors; Sarah Bennet, designer; Wanda Winch,
media researcher; Laura Manthe, production specialist

Photo Credits
By Courtesy of the Bob Hope Memorial Library, Ellis Island, 31; Corbis, 16,
20, Bettmann, 12-13, 40, 41, Minnesota Historical Society, 6, 25 (top), National
Geographic Society/U.S. Government, Justice Immigration and Naturalization
Service, 19; Courtesy of California State Parks, Image 231-18-37, 32, Courtesy of
California State Parks, Image 231-18-13, 26; Courtesy of the National Archives at
Seattle: Exhibit J, Equity Case #40, US Circuit Court in Butte, MT; NAID #298113,
36; CriaImages.com/Jay Robert Nash Collection, 15; Granger, NYC, 11, 39; Library
of Congress: Prints and Photographs Division, cover, 4, 5, 22-23, 24-25, 27, 28-29;
National Parks Service/Colonial National Historical Park/Sidney E. King, artist, 8-9;
Robert M. Bourke, bourkemultimedia.com, 35; Shutterstock: Everett Historical, 42-43,
ilolab, colored texture paper designs, LiliGraphie, vintage photo tab design, vintage
wallpaper, nikoniano, stripe design

TABLE OF CONTENTS

CHAPTER ONE

TO AMERICA

Two young European immigrants stood on the front deck of a steamship, crossing the Atlantic Ocean. Their family had saved up for months to buy them the tickets for their journey. As they looked out over the dark blue water, the sun glistened off the waves. Soon they would arrive in the United States to start a new life. They hoped their lives in America would be better than the ones they left behind.

By the early 1900s, most immigrants came to the United States on steamships.

That desire for a better life is what drove immigration in the early 1900s. People from Europe, Asia, and other parts of the world saved their hard-earned money to purchase tickets to come to America. Many boarded ships with almost nothing in their wallets. They left behind friends, relatives, and neighbors. Some would never see them again. The journey across the ocean was long and scary. They could only hope the risks would be worth it.

Many immigrant families came to the United States looking for a fresh start and new opportunities.

WAVES OF IMMIGRANTS

Millions of people came to the United States in the late 1800s and early 1900s, seeking a new start. America had always been seen as the "land of opportunity." Some immigrants came to find land to farm or better jobs. Some immigrants hoped for the freedom to worship as they wished. Others came to the United States to escape war, **famine**, or cruel governments. And some even came for the adventure a new country offered.

Most immigrants, such as these Russian and Polish immigrants, traveled in the third-class section of the ship known as steerage.

Periods of immigration are called "waves." Like a big wave, the number of people who came to the United States rose up then quieted down again. Around the beginning of the 1900s, the United States experienced the greatest wave of immigration the world has ever seen. But that wasn't the first wave, and it wouldn't be the last.

ᐸᐤ FACT ᐤᐳ

The United States has often been referred to as a "melting pot." The country's population is made up of people from different countries, and they've all added their "flavors" to American culture, while still staying distinctive.

AMERICAN INDIANS

American Indians had lived in America for thousands of years before Europeans arrived. The Europeans' **colonization** of America came at a great price to the Indians. As more people moved in, Indians were pushed off their lands. In 1622 the Powhatan Confederacy nearly wiped out the Jamestown colony to protect their land and way of life. But that solved nothing. Anger and confrontation between immigrant Europeans and Indians only grew as the colonies became the United States. By the 1850s almost all American Indian tribes had been forced onto reservations.

famine—a serious shortage of food resulting in widespread hunger and death
colonization—the settlement of territory by people from another country

Chapter Two

THE FIRST WAVES OF IMMIGRATION

To understand how dramatic immigration in the late 1800s and early 1900s was, it helps to look at previous immigration. The first wave of immigrants ventured to the shores of North America in the late 1500s. At this time European countries such as France, Spain, Holland, and England sent settlers to colonize American territories. In 1607 England founded its first successful community in the Virginia colony. By 1700 nearly 300,000 Europeans were settled in America.

This first wave of immigration peaked around the time of the American Revolution (1775–1783). People from Scotland, Ireland, France, Spain, and Germany flowed into the colonies. After the Revolution, the colonies became the United States of America. Immigrants continued to come to this new country.

SLAVERY IN THE UNITED STATES

The largest group of immigrants to come to America during the first wave was actually slaves from Africa. Slave traders captured men and women in Africa. Then they shipped them to the colonies and forced them into slavery. By 1760 almost 300,000 slaves lived in America. In 1808 Congress made it illegal to bring any more slaves to the states. But by that point, more than 500,000 African people had been forced to come.

HERE COMES ANOTHER WAVE

From 1820 to 1860 another wave of immigration brought more than 7 million people to the United States. These immigrants came mostly from the same European countries as the first wave. Many of these immigrants journeyed to America to escape poverty and famine.

Around 1845 the majority of immigrants coming into America were Irish. At that time Ireland's main source of food was the potato. But a **fungus** began to destroy this important food source. People were starving. Within five years about 1 million Irish people died. Facing starvation, thousands of them left their homes for the United States.

Most of these Irish immigrants had little money when they reached America. Many settled down in cities along the East Coast. A majority of Irish immigrants landed in Boston and stayed. By 1850, 35,000 of Boston's 136,000 residents were Irish immigrants.

Many Irish immigrants fled extreme poverty in Ireland for a chance at a better life in America.

fungus—a single-celled organism that lives by breaking down and absorbing the natural material it lives in

Most Irish were met with hatred when they arrived in the United States. These immigrants were often poor and unskilled. Many American-born people worried the Irish would work for less money and take jobs away from them. Many also feared the Irish would try to push their Catholic religious beliefs on them. Most Irish immigrants had to take jobs that no one else wanted, such as building bridges, roads, and canals.

German rebels raged in the streets of Berlin in March, 1848.

GERMAN IMMIGRATION

The 1850s brought the arrival of nearly 1 million German travelers. These immigrants came to escape disorder within the German government. In 1848 German rebels started a series of revolts to establish a united Germany. But their efforts failed. The rebels feared they would be arrested or attacked for their actions. Between 4,000 and 10,000 of these Germans fled to the United States.

Many of the German immigrants who came to America in the 1850s were highly educated. These people had very different backgrounds from the Germans who came to America in the 1700s. Earlier German immigrants had farming backgrounds. They were drawn to the chance of planting their crops and their futures on American soil. Conflicts between the new German immigrants and the old immigrants were common.

CHINESE IMMIGRATION

The discovery of gold in California in 1848 set off another small wave of immigration. The gold rush attracted immigrants from countries such as France, Germany, Ireland, Mexico, and Chile. But the largest group to come to America for gold was the Chinese. Chinese immigrants called America *gam saan* or "gold mountain."

But gold proved difficult to find. And friendly Americans were few. Like the Irish, most Chinese were not welcomed into the country. Many native-born Americans feared these immigrants would try to destroy the nation's democracy.

Chinese immigrants were often forced to take low-paying, difficult jobs. Some took work in garment factories or as construction workers. Others worked to turn marshes into useable farmland. And a large number of Chinese immigrants took jobs building the **transcontinental** railroad.

Some historians believe as many as 15,000 Chinese worked on the railroad at one time. These workers laid tracks over the Sierra Nevada mountains in extremely cold temperatures and deep snow. They finished the western section of the railroad in 1869, which made travel across the United States possible.

transcontinental—going across a continent

Chapter Three

THE NEW IMMIGRATION

The American Civil War (1861–1865) caused a slow down in immigration. But that slow down did not last long. The largest wave of immigration the world had ever seen was about to roll onto America's shores.

The greatest wave of immigration to America started in 1880 and lasted roughly 40 years. This wave was called the New Immigration. The people who came were called the New Immigrants. It was an amazing period of growth for America. During that time nearly 25 million people journeyed to its shores.

The United States had always been thought of as a land of opportunity. But no time in U.S. history had offered more options to new workers. The nation had recently gone through the Industrial Revolution. Factories now filled cities, creating products quickly and cheaply. And those factories needed workers. The transcontinental railroad made it easy to cross the nation. And the West needed settlers. The country had a stable government that allowed people many freedoms. And for many immigrants, that's just what they were looking for.

New Immigrants often found work in factories such as the Armour and Company meatpacking plant in Chicago.

THE NEW IMMIGRANTS

The majority of immigrants before the New Immigration were northern and western Europeans. The New Immigrants, however, were mostly southern and eastern Europeans. They arrived from places such as Poland, Hungary, Greece, and Italy. In the 1890s more than half a million Italians came to America.

These New Immigrants were young, averaging between 15 and 30 years old. Many spoke no English. The New Immigration also brought more Catholics and Jews to America. Many Jewish immigrants were escaping rising **persecution** in Eastern Europe. More than 2 million Jews came to the United States during this period.

persecution—cruel or unfair treatment, often because of race or religious beliefs

When they entered the country, New Immigrants were given ID tags that corresponded with their ship's passenger list.

COMING FOR A BETTER LIFE

People in the New Immigration wave longed for opportunity, religious and political freedom, and an escape from poverty. German Catholics, Russian Jews, and Polish Jews fled from countries that wouldn't allow them to worship as they wished. Italian immigrants were mostly starving peasants from Southern Italy. In Poland farming jobs were scarce and land ownership was almost impossible. Rumors swirled that jobs and money were everywhere in America. Some even heard that the streets were paved with gold. Life would be easy in America. But for many the reality was quite different. Jobs were not always easy to get because many companies disliked hiring immigrants.

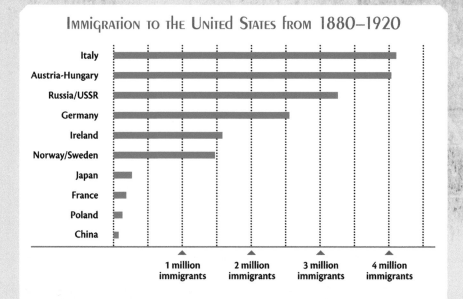

Immigration to the United States from 1880–1920

Italy	████████████████████
Austria-Hungary	███████████████████
Russia/USSR	███████████████
Germany	████████████
Ireland	████████
Norway/Sweden	████████
Japan	██
France	██
Poland	█
China	█

1 million immigrants   2 million immigrants   3 million immigrants   4 million immigrants

Many took hard, dirty work building roads, digging subways, and constructing bridges. Others took work in factories that made them labor long hours in terrible conditions.

Many immigrants took manual labor jobs such as these workers digging the Clinton-Wachusett Sewage System in Massachusetts in 1896.

FASTER SHIPS

Opportunities and freedoms drew many immigrants. But another new development also helped contribute to the incredible number of immigrants. Until the early 1800s, people traveling to America made their voyages on large sailboats. But by the 1840s, steamships that could cruise across oceans began to take control of the seas. These ships were larger, carried more people, and traveled faster. They were also reliable. For the first time in history, ships came and went on regular schedules.

FACT

In the 1880s American railway companies sent agents to European countries to convince immigrant workers to go to America.

FAMOUS IMMIGRANTS

Many of America's most famous people were New Immigrants. Composer Irving Berlin came to New York from Russia in 1893. He would go on to write famous songs such as "White Christmas" and "God Bless America." Harry Houdini traveled to America from Hungary at the very start of the New Immigration wave. He later became the world's most famous magician. Max Factor was a Russian immigrant who arrived in 1906. He ended up creating one of the most famous makeup companies in the world.

SETTLING IN

Most of the New Immigrants made their homes in the northern cities of the East Coast, such as New York. Many simply could not afford to move away. Others found comfort living in **urban** neighborhoods with other immigrants from their home countries. Italians quickly filled the streets of Lower Manhattan. In some cases people from the same Italian village all lived on the same block or in the same **tenement**.

urban—having to do with a city
tenement—a rundown apartment building

Many immigrants did move westward, though. Those immigrants traveled farther west to buy their own farmland. Roughly half of all the German immigrants who arrived during the New Immigration moved to the Midwest for farming. Many of those who came from Sweden and Norway traveled to Minnesota and the Dakota territories to settle land. The increase of people in Dakota territory allowed that area to become the states of North and South Dakota in 1889.

Many immigrants in Minnesota and the Dakota territories built log cabins from the bountiful timber in the area.

Taken in 1900, this photograph shows Mulberry Street in New York City. This street was often considered the main street of little Italy, where many Italian immigrants lived.

Angel Island, California, was the western entry point for many immigrants, such as these Asian immigrants in 1925.

IMMIGRATION IN THE WEST

During the New Immigration, the largest number of immigrants went to the East Coast of the United States. But a large number of Asian immigrants arrived in the West. In the early 1900s, Japan's population was growing quickly. To provide for the growing number of people, factories sprang up. But the factories were built on farmland, pushing farmers out of their jobs. More than 100,000 Japanese immigrants came to America between 1900 and 1925. Many hoped to find land to farm in the wide-open United States.

Japanese immigrants arrived on America's West Coast and settled in California. Many found work on the railroad or in lumber mills, mining camps, and **canneries**. However most were farmers. Japanese farmers often rented land and small cabins out in the country. They started farms, orchards, and vineyards. By 1920 Japanese immigrants controlled 450,000 acres (182,109 hectares) of land in California.

cannery—a factory where food is put into cans

MEXICAN IMMIGRATION

There was also a surge in immigration from Mexico at the beginning of the 20th century. These hopefuls came for economic opportunities as well. Most of these immigrants did not travel into America through a port city. Instead, they walked into the country through Texas. More than 500,000 Mexican immigrants officially entered by 1930. But Mexico borders the United States. Many people came to the country to work and then returned to their homes. There is no way to know how many Mexican immigrants settled permanently in the United States during this time.

Many Mexican immigrants worked on farms doing the back-breaking work of picking vegetables and fruits such as canteloupe melons.

Chapter Four

ENTERING THE COUNTRY

✺ FACT ✺

Approximately 40 percent of U.S. citizens today can trace their roots back to an immigrant who came through Ellis Island.

Opened in 1855, Castle Garden was New York City's initial immigrant processing center. It was closed on April 18, 1890, when the federal government took over the processing of immigrants. This adjustment would forever change immigrants' experience of arriving in America.

In 1892 the federal government opened a New Immigrant processing center called Ellis Island. From 1892 to 1924, more than 12 million hopeful arrivals passed into America through its halls. Ellis Island has become a symbol of the American immigrant experience. It was called the "Island of Hope, Island of Tears," since arriving was such an emotional experience.

ELLIS ISLAND

At Ellis Island immigrants went through an inspection process. Inspectors checked to make sure each person was healthy. They also checked to make sure immigrants weren't criminals. The inspections took anywhere from three to seven hours. Immigrants who were sick were **quarantined** and treated until they were better. Then they were allowed into the United States.

Some immigrants were sent back to the countries they came from due to illness or criminal records. But those people were few. Most immigrants were able to get through inspection and start their new lives. About 98 percent of the people who passed through were allowed entry into America.

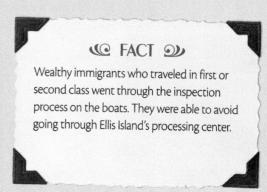

⟪☚ FACT ☚⟫

Wealthy immigrants who traveled in first or second class went through the inspection process on the boats. They were able to avoid going through Ellis Island's processing center.

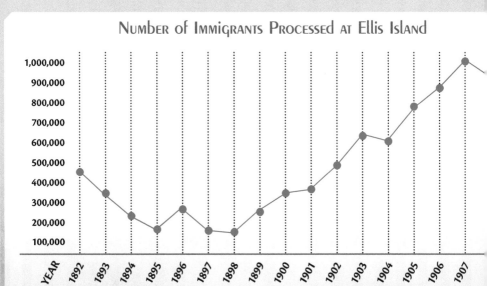

Number of Immigrants Processed at Ellis Island

quarantine—to keep a person away from others to stop a disease from spreading

STATUE OF LIBERTY

To get to Ellis Island, ships passed Liberty Island and its famous Statue of Liberty. The Statue of Liberty was a gift to the United States from France. For immigrants who floated past her on their way to Ellis Island, the Statue of Liberty was a beautiful symbol of the freedoms and opportunities they hoped to find in America.

Weary travelers waited in long lines as immigration officials on Ellis Island processed thousands of New Immigrants per day.

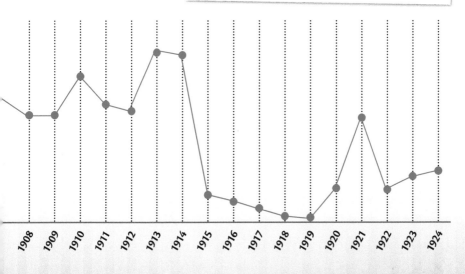

http://www.nps.gov/elis/forteachers/upload/Statistics.pdf

ANGEL ISLAND

Asian immigrants coming to the West Coast were processed through Angel Island near San Francisco, California. Immigrants there had a very different experience than those processed at Ellis Island. Federal laws limited the number of Chinese and Japanese immigrants who were allowed into the country. Some hopeful immigrants waited months on the island before being sent home or being allowed entry.

Immigrants at Angel Island were not treated well. Officials at Angel Island sent back as many Asian immigrants as possible. At the time an idea called **nativism** was popular in America. Nativism is the belief that people born in a country are better than immigrants. This idea affected the way people treated newcomers, and it even influenced the laws passed by Congress.

Angel Island immigration officers process papers for one Asian man and several Asian women in 1925.

nativism—a movement that reflected preferences for native-born Americans and mistrust of immigrants

CHAPTER FIVE

NATIVISM

Immigrants came to the United States by the thousands. These new people brought their languages, customs, and histories with them. The differences added richness to the U.S. culture. But some people were uncomfortable with these differences.

Nativism didn't start with the New Immigrants. Irish immigrants in the mid-1800s experienced it. Nativists attacked Irish immigrants with words and fists. In 1844 anti-immigrant mobs in Philadelphia and other East Coast cities attacked the homes of Irish immigrants. Landlords refused to let Irish live in their buildings. Shop owners denied Irish jobs in their factories.

The anti-immigrant sentiment was focused on Irish immigrants in the northeast. This artist's rendering captured a common sight on businesses in the late 1800s and early 1900s.

"No Irish Need Apply"

Anonymous (Written about 1910)

NATIVISM AND THE LAW

By 1882 Chinese immigrants had taken jobs in factories, on farms, and on railroads in the West. Many U.S. citizens feared Chinese laborers were taking too many American jobs. Congress passed the Chinese Exclusion Act, making it illegal for more Chinese to come to America.

BOYCOTT

A General Boycott has been declared upon all CHINESE and JAPANESE Restaurants, Tailor Shops and Wash Houses. Also all persons employing them in any capacity.

All Friends and Sympathizers of Organized Labor will assist us in this fight against the lowering Asiatic standards of living and of morals.

AMERICA vs. ASIA
Progress vs. Retrogression
Are the considerations involved.

BY ORDER OF
Silver Bow Trades and Labor Assembly
and Butte Miners' Union

Unions organized to oppose Asian businesses and workers.

Many Chinese men immigrated to the United States in search of gold, leaving their families behind. The Chinese Exclusion Act made it impossible for those families to reunite in America. It also made it nearly impossible for immigrants to visit China and then return to the states.

In 1907 the U.S. and Japanese governments agreed to slow immigration from Japan. Japanese immigrants had been flowing in, looking for farmland and good jobs. But again, Americans' attitudes turned to anger. The Japanese government wanted to keep good relations between the two countries. It agreed to deny passports to citizens who wanted to go to the United States. This pact became known as the "Gentleman's Agreement."

IMMIGRATION ACT OF 1924

By the 1920s nativism had become widespread in the country. A growing number of Americans feared immigrants would take over and change their way of life. To please these people, Congress passed a law that would change immigration in America forever. On April 12, 1924, Congress passed the Immigration Act of 1924. This law created a **quota** system, limiting the total number of people who could be admitted into the country. The law said that no more than 150,000 immigrants could enter the United States each year. The Immigration Act effectively ended the New Immigration.

FACT

Under the Immigration Act of 1924, Asian immigrants were still not allowed into the states. The Chinese Exclusion Act was in effect until 1943. The ban on Japanese immigration wasn't lifted until 1952.

quota—a fixed number of something

Chapter Six

CHANGING AMERICAN LIFE

The beginning of the 1900s saw the peak of New Immigration. But rising nativism, new laws, and the start of World War I (1914–1918) caused U.S. immigration to decline. Almost 10 million people arrived on America's shores from 1900 to 1910. But in the next decade, that number was reduced by almost half. Fewer than 1 million immigrants entered the country in the 1930s.

America's burst of growth from the New Immigration had come to an end. But the effects of the wave were amazing. Roughly 50 million people lived in the United States in 1880. In 1920, 100 million people called America home. With the help of the New Immigration, the United States' population had nearly doubled.

☜ FACT ☞

By 1900 New York City housed more Italians than any city but Rome, Italy. As many Irish lived there as there were in Dublin, Ireland. And more Jews lived in New York City than in any other city in the world.

The New Immigration wave overlapped with a period of industrial and economic growth resulting in booming American cities such as New York City.

39

CHANGED ECONOMY

The enormous number of people who came to the United States during the New Immigration wave changed the country forever. At the start of the wave, farming was America's main industry. But by the end, manufacturing provided just as many jobs as farming. This shift happened because a growing population had a growing need for tools, food, clothes—anything people needed. And that meant more jobs to make those products.

The Ford Motor Company in Highland Park, Michigan, was the first factory to employ the assembly line to create its goods.

Mexican orange workers gathered at a political rally in Los Angeles, California, in 1936.

POLITICS AND POPULAR CULTURE

New Immigrants also played an important role in shaping the government, music, and art in the country. Immigrants came with differing ideas of how a government should be run. Immigrants led unions that fought for fair working conditions and pay for all American workers. Their children grew up to be the nation's new lawmakers and voters.

Immigrants also shaped the American creative arts. Many immigrants and their children became writers, directors, and actors. Others wrote Broadway plays that are still popular today. They communicated their beliefs and feelings through the arts. Their popular films and songs influenced American culture.

A NATION OF IMMIGRANTS

Since its beginning, the United States has been a land of immigrants. Starting in the 1500s, people left their homes for the opportunities they hoped to find on America's shores. The huge numbers of immigrants in the early 1900s flooded the country with fresh workers, new ideas, and different ways of life. America was shaped by all those who made the journey. The different languages, beliefs, skin colors, and cultures created a country rich with diversity.

43

TIMELINE

1607

English colonists found Jamestown, the first successful community in the Virginia colony.

1622

The Powhatan Confederacy nearly wipes out the Jamestown Colony in an attempt to protect its lands.

1775–1783

During the American Revolution a first wave of immigration to America reaches its peak.

1808

Congress makes it illegal to bring more slaves to the states.

1820–1860

The United States experiences another wave of immigration. More than 7 million people come to the country.

1840

Companies begin using steamships to travel across oceans. These new ships allow for faster and more reliable trips.

1845–1849

Ireland's potato crops are destroyed by a fungus. The Irish Potato Famine causes millions of Irish citizens to move away, many to the United States.

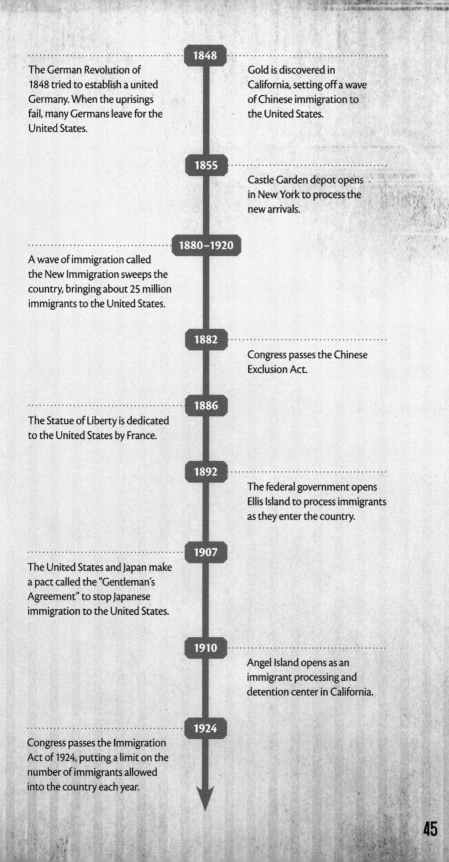

1848

The German Revolution of 1848 tried to establish a united Germany. When the uprisings fail, many Germans leave for the United States.

Gold is discovered in California, setting off a wave of Chinese immigration to the United States.

1855

Castle Garden depot opens in New York to process the new arrivals.

1880–1920

A wave of immigration called the New Immigration sweeps the country, bringing about 25 million immigrants to the United States.

1882

Congress passes the Chinese Exclusion Act.

1886

The Statue of Liberty is dedicated to the United States by France.

1892

The federal government opens Ellis Island to process immigrants as they enter the country.

1907

The United States and Japan make a pact called the "Gentleman's Agreement" to stop Japanese immigration to the United States.

1910

Angel Island opens as an immigrant processing and detention center in California.

1924

Congress passes the Immigration Act of 1924, putting a limit on the number of immigrants allowed into the country each year.

GLOSSARY

cannery (KAN-ur-ee)—a factory where food is put into cans

colonization (kah-luh-ni-ZAY-shun)—the settlement of territory by people from another country; the new settlement is controlled by that county

famine (FA-muhn)—a serious shortage of food resulting in widespread hunger and death

fungus (FUHN-guhs)—a single-celled organism that lives by breaking down and absorbing the natural material it lives in

nativism (NAY-tuh-viz-uhm)—a movement that reflected preferences for native-born Americans and mistrust of immigrants

persecution (pur-suh-CUE-shun)—cruel or unfair treatment, often because of race or religious beliefs

quarantine (KWOR-uhn-teen)—to keep a person, animal, or plant away from others to stop a disease from spreading

quota (KWOH-tuh)—a fixed number of something

tenement (TEN-uh-muhnt)—a rundown apartment building, especially one that is crowded and in a poor part of a city

transcontinental (transs-kon-tuh-NEN-tuhl)—extending or going across a continent

urban (UR-bun)—having to do with a city

READ MORE

Benoit, Peter. *Immigration*. Cornerstones of Freedom. New York: Children's Press, 2012.

Harrison, Geoffrey, and Thomas F. Scott. *New Americans*. Great Debates. Chicago: Norwood House Press, 2014.

Marcovitz, Hal. *Ellis Island: The Story of a Gateway to America*. Patriotic Symbols of America. Philadelphia: Mason Crest, 2015.

CRITICAL THINKING USING THE COMMON CORE

Using other texts, explore how nativism shaped the government and culture in the United States. Are there any examples of nativism today? *(Integration of Knowledge and Ideas)*

What effect did the invention of steamships have on immigration to the United States? *(Key Ideas and Details)*

INTERNET SITES

FactHound offers a safe, fun way to find Internet sites related to this book. All of the sites on FactHound have been researched by our staff.

Here's all you do:
Visit *www.facthound.com*
Type in this code: 9781491441268

INDEX